WE STILL BE

Poems and Performances

Careful memoir meets granite manifesto in this brilliant collection of wordplay. Through the doors of these poems, you get the sense for the true scope of the people; the ocean of the people; the countless biographies behind each marching eye in the city. And as we battle for the soul of metropolises ever turned against us, Flores is a poet frontline; proving that in craft is ascension.

—Tongo Eisen-Martin, San Francisco Poet Laureate, author and activist

WE STILL BE is a raised fist. It is an open heart. It is a vulnerable love letter to place, pain, and permanence. Flores is a street prophet. A 21st Century Tlatoani. A flor y canto culture-bearer who invites us into the temple and psyche of the highbrow-hood. Through barrio analysis, academic insight, unyielding empathy, and profound introspection, *WE STILL BE* implores us to see, acknowledge, and tell the truth. These extremely personal palabras, prayers, and performances examine and interrogate the complexities of identity and celebrate the power of collective resilience. In a world that is obsessed with our erasure, this bold collection is a monument—a camino of cuentos that read like a litany of ritual, reminding us that WE STILL BE!

—Bobby LeFebre, Colorado Poet Laureate, writer, performer, cultural worker

"Paul S. Flores is incomparable in his tenacity and perseverance to bring our stories to life with his writings and poetry. All our complexities as a Latinx community are captured in this book. Our culture is embedded in his soul and *WE STILL BE* grateful that Flores continues to inspire and innovate with such passion. ¡Siempre pa'lante!"

—Emanuel Xavier, author & activist

WE STILL BE

Poems and Performances

by

Paul S. Flores

EL MARTILLO PRESS

EL MARTILLO PRESS

WE STILL BE: Poems and Performances by Paul S. Flores.
©Paul S. Flores, 2023. All rights reserved.

ISBN: 978-1-0881-1777-4

Published by El Martillo Press
in the United States of America.
elmartillopress.com

Cover by Xavi Moreno.
iamxavi.com

Set in Garamond.
Typeset for El Martillo Press by David A. Romero.
davidaromero.com

NOTICE: SCHOOLS AND BUSINESSES
El Martillo Press offers copies of this book at quantity discount with bulk purchase for educational, business, or sales promotional use. For information, please email the publisher at elmartillopress@gmail.com.

For my anchors and my good luck charms. For my angels, my gitanas and my roots. For Iyalorde. For Egun. Con la bendición de todos mi ancestros. Aché.

For Christina

All my heart and soul

11/20/23

Ava

For Christine

Work on

All my

Best

11/20/22
USA

CONTENTS

WE STILL BE
21ˢᵗ Century Performance Poems

CHICANO SUPERNOVA

Spanglish

I unearth my mother's tongue
and hold it in my hand like a flopping fish
a gleaming survivor

I remember my first dance around the kitchen table
Beny Moré was singing on Mexican radio
Castellano que bueno baila usted
The double meaning at play
Castellano is the original name for Spanish
My grandmother was dancing
She said, "Agarreme por los hips."
I did/She led
and my first movement was Spanglish

It's got nothing to do with my broad back
or my ability to endure hard labor
I'm not an unusual Mexican for being intelligent
My social consciousness is complex
Out of necessity we moved
from one nation to another
from one language to another
from one identity into another
And when I found my lover
she reminded me of my mother—
because Spanglish people
recognize the Spanglish experience in each other

So, I roll my R's like roles
Cinco con guacamole

I blow lights out on the border
Shine 'em on mi lenguaje
I swim in this cultural molasses
If I'm pure anything, homie
soy puro Spanglish

More than a simple combination of idioms,
this reality we witness and create
My grandmother never learned to speak proper English,
but she taught me to dance on the hyphen
between Mexican-Cuban-American
between roots and assimilation
congas y trompetas
corn and harina
so that it all looks like one movement

Castellano que bueno baila usted
The double meaning at play
when everything is multicultural
but America remains monolingual

I mean, if everybody loves
to wrap their favorite condiments in a tortilla
then why don't they call it a burrito?
Instead of Mexicano-Chicano
they refer to us as Those People

Those people are always fighting
Those people are always drinking
Those people are always having so many babies
Those people can't even speak English right

We've built a tolerance for ignorance
but it's the myth of superiority
that I can't stomach

From Ricky Ricardo
to Ritchie Valenz
to Ricky Martin
we want to be accepted
But we're too brown
for whites, and too raro
for real Mexicans
Even Selena was forced to learn
traditional Mexican music
when racist Texans rejected her rock 'n roll

Spanglish is unorthodox
No one can understand us
but us outcast mestizos
congri de cristianos y moros
gallo pinto con huevo
Buenas noches, criollo!

Spanglish is the echo
from my grandmother's kitchen
My interpretation of a reality
that ignores our contributions

Spanglish is what I do
to reflect my mix

But this ain't no new marketing gimmick
No new stereotype

Mixing cultures can be hazardous
when reality is black and white

Castellano que bueno baila usted
The double meaning at play
So, I roll my R's like roles
Cinco con guacamole
I blow lights out on the border
Shine 'em on me language
I swim in this cultural molasses
If I'm pure anything, homie
Soy puro Spanglish

Crowbar Thing

At the height of the San Francisco Dot Com "boom," Peter Glikshtern, owner of the popular Liquid Bar on 16th Street, beat and seriously injured three Latino immigrants with a crowbar who had been drinking at his club. The event ignited feelings of violence and racism attached to the gentrification of the Mission, especially after Glikshtern was cleared of all charges.

Can I ask you a question?
Are you doing that crowbar thing?
Liquid thing, 16th Street Corridor crawl thing, that grimy thing
That thing about being hip without trying too hard, that whole
      ironic thing
About telling him, telling her, telling us, telling them that we
must clean up the Mission because cool people need a cool
      place to drink thing
A lookin' for a good time thing, an' I'm tired of the Marina
      thing
A Polaroid postcard crackhead and prostitute thing
A hipsters in the dicey barrio thing
An' it's just like the Lower East Side thing,
graffiti on the front door, hot music, and cool DJs thing
An opportunistic—I mean optimistic thing because can't you
      see the benefit of more
green space and bike lane thing
Besides, how could gentrification be violent if artists started it?

Are you doing that crowbar thing?

The cash in your Oracle stock and buy a bar in the Mission
      thing
The protect your investment, even if it means displacement
      thing
The it's not personal, strictly business thing
The just trying to live the American Dream thing
The white man's burden thing
The new sheriff in town thing
The show 'em your gun thing
The violence and destitution is so sexy thing
The civilize the savages thing
The vigilante thing
The cross and the crowbar thing
The Arnold Schwarzenegger thing

Are you doing that crowbar thing?

That English Only thing
That snitch to la migra when you can't stand your Latino
      clients or employees thing
That drug dealers, prostitutes, and Mexicans are all the same
      thing
That electronic hate mail thing
That reverse racism thing
That hijole thing
That no mames, guey thing
That que tu esperabas thing
That Mexican beer is better at room temperature thing
That Glikshtern club-hopping, immigrant crowbar bashing
      thing

Are you doing that crowbar thing?

Doing the forget about the Centro del Pueblo thing
Doing the volunteer at The Pirate Store instead thing
Doing the post-Chicano thing because I'm not political, I'm an
    artist thing
Doing the more green spaces thing because murals don't
    prevent violence thing
Doing the bike lane thing because lowriders aren't ecologically
    beneficial thing
Doing the save the whales thing because my parents graduated
    from Berkeley thing
Doing the indie rock thing because hip-hop is so misogynistic
    now thing
Doing that retro 80s thing because I got bigger fish to fry so I
    gotta get mine thing
Doing the righteous thing because sometimes immigrants
    deserve to get beat in the head with a crowbar thing

Besides, how could gentrification be violent if artists started it?

Are you doing that crowbar thing?

Chicano Supernova

Leaving behind a black thread of asphalt tied to San Francisco's international orange doorknob, the poet-pied piper of the Chicano hormiga supernova rolls through the northern vineyards in his '66 Chevy, bumping the new Jay-Z, windows up, as the temperature outside the city limits climbs twenty-five degrees. Roll the windows down and breathe. Instead of glory, he sees crosses in the peach orchards, crosses in the grape vines, crosses in the strawberry fields. Cross-rows of service and rejection where martyrs became co-opted by Apple, Inc. while the suburbs became the city.

He knows what he will find in Santa Rosa. The same thing he found in Pittsburg, in Modesto and Vallejo. Barrio youth that used to live in the Mission District of San Francisco forced out, back the way their parents came when they immigrated. Used to participate in the inner-city summer art camp. Used to take samba, capoeira, and sugar skull classes at the cultural center. Were on their way as future artistas of la Galería de la Raza. Could have continued emblazoning murals of peace over the City's amplified homicide statistics and increased the documentary videos of youth dignity. But now they reside in a low-income housing complex in Santa Rosa's Apple Valley.

Here the poet pied piper of the Chicano hormiga supernova will find sixteen ambivalently suspicious young raza faces ringed with orange detritus of government-subsidized Hot Cheetos. Sixteen pre-teens, tweeners, and teenagers, plus a few adult supervisors, barely eighteen but wiser beyond their years, synthesized and edited into a municipal trailer crammed with a foosball table and broken computers, a stereo surround sound big screen TV with a PlayStation connection and Wii handy, low rider and tattoo graphics pinned to the blue upholstered walls like set decoration for the Laugh Now, Cry Later tour.

This is a tiny trailer that serves as a rec center fifty miles north of the Mission, and I'm the poet trying not to show less than a professional touch. This is my first day of a residency that's supposed to last a month. It's hard to imagine how an MFA I'm still paying for got me this far. But after driving for an hour, I don't have time to think how I feel a little depressed about the surroundings of my stage and audience, so I project an alter-ego everybrownman superhero character and start to bust. Not knowing how many speak Spanish or English, I trust when they hear something in either one, they'll let it be known whether they like it or not. Then mouth holes drop like dominos into laughter, confusion, boredom, and astonishment over thirty minutes of spoken Spanglish Bay Area love notes delivered in mesmerizing rhythm and flavor. They want to recite my lyrics with me. So, the heavy metal and professional wrestling fans tell me, "Do it again! Represent! ¡Representa!"

But my purpose isn't just a performance to watch. So, we make dialogue out of it. I ask them to write about the difference between the way the world sees them and how they see themselves by comparing their identities to the day and night, and then excuse myself to use the restroom. Come to find out it's a port-a-potty outside around back. The city hasn't fixed the bathrooms in the trailer for over a month, and I wonder how they had money to pay for my presentation but not repair the toilets. Needless to say, the port-a-potty is shitty, smeared and wack. I can't use it. No wonder out of a project of four hundred residents only fifteen youth came to hear me rap. Outside I stare through a large hole in the chain link fence. Past the train tracks a pair of grape pickers carrying Kendall-Jackson sacks piss under a tree. But, I decide not to act in accordance and wait until the second hour is up so I can drive away to relieve myself. I slowly walk back into the trailer more determined to hear what my writers came up with.

Rosie says, "By day I am a momma polar bear on the melting ice and home is further and further away. My father got stopped by ICE again on the way home from work yesterday. They would have took his car if he'd been driving without his license. He knows never to leave home without it. But I was born in San Francisco. No one there ever stopped me or my family for being Latino. Now my dad drives a truck and we live in Rosetown. Everyone thinks we're immigrants. But we can't be deported. The boys here are rude and when I wear blue to school, they call me a scrap. I used to play the clarinet at International Studies Academy, but now I can't concentrate. By day I am knocking Tupac hard in my iPhone Mini. I can't take this country life shit. I went from hip-hop thugs to cowboys in rat skin boots. By night I sing the blues to my friends on Snapchat. I don't study math or history. Instead, I download ringtones to personalize my cell phone, and daydream about when we can move back to San Francisco. But I might have to repeat 9th grade. I'm not dumb, there's just no one to talk to."

When she reads it out loud there's a discomfort across the board, faces betraying an unfortunate feeling of guilt, or anxiety at being the next one called on to read. Not everyone comes as honest as Rosie, but most see a need to express anger and frustration with their identity. Some struggle with writing in English. A few laugh it off with gangster fronts of, "Oh, that's gay. Why you crying?" trying to tell me they don't care. But I know mythologizing their reality is the only way some can deal with the fact that dad is in prison and mom can't read. Is it just young people's angst, or is it a cultural creep? Before our rites of passage were junior high school crushes, sports, and weed. Now it's claiming sets, sex and ecstasy, juvenile hall and ICE raids, all before you turn thirteen. And that's when I make everyone stand in a circle to stretch their voice. First, we whisper, then we scream.

On the way back to the City, the dome of the SF Palace of Fine Arts preens a red terracotta monument of classic Western accomplishment. I realize there's no protection from feeling like poverty awaits you. Even though right now you may have a home there is still no guarantee someone isn't scheming to take it all away. We may not like it, but they stuck us in this predicament together, citizens and immigrants chasing the American Dream. Even though we got different issues, we take different avenues, we end up dumped in the same housing project, classroom, prison cell, parking lot, and lettuce field. The poet pied piper of the Chicano hormiga supernova is no exception. But the price of gas is going higher, and the people are being spread out further from the center. I gotta get a map of suburbia and hope that BART will soon reach Santa Rosa.

Brown Dreams

Inspired by Jorge Mariscal and Richard Rodriguez

This is a true story
about a brown dream
sinking to the bottom of the Tigris-Euphrates

This is a brown dream.

It was Francisco's last night out with his friends.
Three of them on their way to see the latest sci-fi movie.
They were driving.
A stereo jocking the latest top 40 rapper,
because that was all he listened to.
But it didn't matter.

Music was only part of the setting
and not the motivation for late night
brainstorms about how to make money,
or how to escape the feeling of being
left out of a dream so many painted
red, white, and blue.

But his dream was brown.
Brown as his skin.
Brown and impure.
Brown as Eve's apple after she took the first bite.
Brown as the everlasting blur of English, African, and Indian
moving through the forests of this continent
four hundred years ago
before it was known as destiny.

Before he had ever heard the word
"immigrant"
Beaner! Spic! Stupid! Dirty!
Before he had ever dreamt of assimilation.

He is 18 and Mexican.
He is in San Diego,
Topeka, Buffalo, San Antonio,
Oakland, California.
He wants a piece of the American Dream.

Francisco wanted a college degree.
He wanted to be a stockbroker, or FBI agent,
because those were the jobs with the most power.
If he could have been a rock star or a superhero
there would have been no need to enlist.
But he had to be a U.S. citizen
if he was going to make a living like them.

The Army recruiter at his high school
told him that if he served in the military
he could automatically become a U.S. citizen.
After four years duty and an honorable discharge
there would be plenty of money left over
for him to continue his education
at a good institution.
Or he could take his technical skills
as a tank operator or small weapons expertise
and apply them to a civilian job.

It was exciting;
Brown boy who wasn't even a citizen,

who had barely been a resident five years,
who didn't know much about education,
was now willing to die to become a student.

One year later
he was working on a tank unit
fighting in Iraq.
Francisco heard it was the second time
the president had invaded this nation.
They were driving in the desert.
They were taking fire, swerving.
The tank lost control
and headed straight into the river.

As Francisco's lungs filled up with water
he remembered his last night out with his friends;
How his mother had wanted to cook dinner for him—
but he didn't want to spend another hour
in that cramped apartment
where she cooked for six of his brothers,
his two uncles and their compadres.
Instead, Francisco invited Jose and Diego
out to the movies
because that's what Americans did.

Now his soul is an ancestor in the Euphrates.
Chicano blood mixing with Arab soil,
returning to the Garden of Eden
by way of the U.S. Army,
same way it had come.

Only now, he would finally receive something
he had been promised:
An officially-sealed envelope on top of Old Glory.
Citizenship had never been earned so graciously.
Even, if it comes posthumously—
Why don't they extend it to the victim's family?

The American Dream is dirty.
Why should Chicanos have to die
to earn the approval of this society?

This is a brown dream.
Brown as the bus riders union.
Brown as gasoline.
Brown as the Tigris-Euphrates
The Mississippi, and the Rio Grande.
Brown as coyotes.
Brown as the blood-soaked sands of Iraq
and on the ranches of Arizona border vigilantes.
Brown as Affirmative Action in the military
but not the university.
This is a brown dream.

Sidewalk Librarian

I got Daisy Zamora
Giaconda Bellí, and Claribel Alegría

You
wanna buy some poetry?
I got Claribel Alegría
"Yo estuve mucho rato en el chorro del río."
You ever read that before?

You think I'm crazy like that dude
who stands in the doorway of the furniture store
on Valencia Street with his guitar
looking like John Cougar Mellencamp on crack
Don't you?

You are looking at my library, baby.
I will trade you a book for a burrito,
or piece of pan dulce.

The Central American poets taught me
about surviving with dignity
Do you understand me?
I ain't trying to sell poetry to nostalgic-minded immigrants.
No, honey. They don't need reminding.

I got history.
When I was younger, San Francisco was alive with Revolution.

We started student strikes,
and held up banks to post bail
for Huey Newton and Bobby Seale.
People hijacking planes to Cuba.
We had Assata. She was the Revolution.
We had Audre Lorde. She was the Revolution.
We had Lolita Lebron. She was the Revolution.

I am a strong woman.
I am still the revolution.

What you got here now?
"Los que no tienen patria, ni nación.
Sino solo una finca."
Folks with no history, no country.
Just real estate.
Roque Dalton said that.

> I want to walk with a bone through my hair
> Teased out, and naked
>   —except for a loincloth
> Declaiming the poetry of my ancestors
> with a spear in my hand
> Gathering the kin together to tell the story of our
>   migration
> The wars we courageously fought, the songs we sing
> the livestock we own and the tapestries we make

I want to represent my tribe with property.
Wouldn't that be something?
If I stood out here and told the truth
        …about property

Wouldn't that be real?

You wanna buy some poetry?
Everyone wants to live in a loft
with big windows.
Like a big fishbowl.

Shoot, I want to live in one, too.
I want to live in one of them lofts.
So, all of you can watch me be rich.
Watch me go up and down the staircase
Watch what kind of furniture I lounge in
What kind of computer I have

I got Daisy Zamora,
Giaconda Bellí, and Claribel Alegría...

You a businessman under that goatee?
Gonna get your eyelids tattooed?
Want your private parts pierced at Body Manipulations?

Listen, honey.
I got a jaguar tattooed on my soul.
My lips been pierced by a quetzal feather
dipped in America's veins.
I used it to spell my name
on a check for forty acres and a mule.
The bank took my picture,
xeroxed and posted it.
It was performance art.

Hold your wallet close 'round here.
Treat it like an anchor.
Otherwise, you might start to believe
what I got is really worth something.
You might could buy yourself a clue!

If you're an undercover type fella
we got plenty of other games to play.
Around the corner is Oliver North's cousin
He got contraband from Iran.

As a matter of fact...
Here.
Give him one of these.
Pobrecito.
Remember to tell him I sent you.

Today, it's free.
And if you don't like that book
I'll give you your money back.
Guaranteed.

I got Daisy Zamora,
Giaconda Bellí, and Claribel Alegría...

Arroz Con Pollo

Come to my house for dinner, compa
Estamos cocinando
Arroz con pollo
Tostones
Frijoles negros

We'll have antojitos
on red mantos
Mojitos to brighten
your mente with mint
Tune your ear to clave
Clap on your lap
Lightly and on time
like ajo and lime
on everything

We will greet you with
the scent of warm olive oil and garlic
Roasted red and green pepper
sautéed with onion,
cumin and oregano
The aroma will primp your appetite
Make you want to pasear
Chat at the lip of a ventana
Feel the coquettish breeze
Admire palm leaves that
Wave like sabanas in the wind

Ahora sí, asere
Te invito a mi casa
Plantains mashed by hand
rubbed like fingers over a cajón
We use paper
Not a tostonera
Because we like tostones thin

Black beans soaking overnight
softening
to your taste
Frijoles negros
so sweet with red wine vinegar
and rum
they even simmered
in the muanga of Orquesta Aragón

Come to my house for dinner, mi herma
Seguro que
we won't disappoint you
Tonight, my señorita's cooking
arroz con pollo
estilo Cubano
so exquisite
so delicious
so perfect
Because she is the one
who makes this dish
a reflection of her soul

Golden
rice moist

but not wet
con guisantes and Spanish chorizo
Roasting, frying, and baking
Ese chicken
rubbed with paprika
para que te pica
Spice in the bite
sharp and crisp

Como café
despues de una siesta
Awake in the tastes and textures
Open your palette
like windows open
on humid green mountainside

Come share the table with us
Savor the cuisine
¡Hay ambiente!
Must be a celebration
I made this poem
to be like an invitation
So, bring your lover
bring your brother
and bring your mother
Because this is a meal
you will want to remember

Gravity's Volume: Black & Brown

For Geoffrey Canada and Luis J. Rodriguez

I work in East Oakland. I carry a briefcase and codeswitch for a paycheck, pushing Black and Brown equity at meetings with deputy superintendents, regional taskforces and symposiums on structural racism and violence prevention.

I be in these meetings talking about systems.

The gravity of Black boys in these systems is nothing like Newton's apple. The gravity is more like the Grim Reaper's sickle. Maybe that's why the street signs in East Oakland sometimes look like tombstones.

1 in 3 will be incarcerated
7 out of 10 will fall into recidivism
25% survive on $10,000 a year
Half won't graduate high school
35% are unemployed
16 times more likely than white boys to die from homicide

The gravity...

For the first time ever in Oakland Latinos are the majority in public schools. We have the highest birth rates, eclipse all ethnicities in the state. But severely disproportionate to graduation rates. Schools be hostile like the Alamo. No translation services. Mamá's request to speak to the principal falls on monolingual ears. *Wait here, please.* Her cultura held hostage by bankrupt state policies and disrespected by an incompetent curriculum and culturally chauvinistic administrators. She becomes deaf to the system. Her babies cry for attention by waving gang signs.

The volume...

I be in these meetings talking about systems.

I'm often the only Latino in a room full of Black friends. I'm often the only Latino in a room full of White friends. And if someone decides to call me *hermano*; ask me what Latinos think of Obama; or where they can get the best steak burrito in Oakland—I say that steak is *carne asada*. I tell them to go to El Ojo De Agua taco truck on Fruitvale Ave. Because I represent my *raza*. It's what we all want: To represent.

Then I say: The volume is rising. Listen! We been saying the same thing for 10 years. The system is a placebo. An inertia. Apathetic. I've even busted poems in these meetings. I even busted poems in these meetings... but all I hear is business cards dancing on gravity.

The fact is Black boys are at the bottom of every measure of success, every standard of achievement, every level of society. If the gravity of their situation don't move you to do something different, then the volume of Brown demographics are gonna hit you like a tsunami.

So, when we say Black and Brown Unity what could we be
    talking about?
Our issues with good hair and bad hair?
Pelo bueno, pelo malo?

Do we all just need to learn to speak American?
America. Yes. The continent.

The first recorded African slave uprising in the Americas happened in México in 1546.

The first African free pueblo in the hemisphere was founded and named after Yanga, an African prince, freed slave in Veracruz, México in 1609.

Mexico's second president, Vicente Ramon Guerrero was an African-Mexican who abolished slavery in 1829.

During the US-Mexican war of 1848 Mexicans refused to force runaway slaves back to their US slave masters, and so México lost half her territory.

Mexican and African. Black and Brown. These brothers enjoy a rich legacy of alliance. But we don't teach that in school. We don't celebrate it in the workplace. So, Black and Brown don't see each other as equal.

In 1965, African-Americans celebrated the Voting Rights Act that ended Jim Crow pre-requisites to vote. At the same time, Chicanos began the Delano Grape Strike and for the first time Mexican-Americans grabbed the national spotlight. Today there are more than 200 public schools, 500 streets throughout the country named after Martin Luther King, Jr. and Cesar Chavez.

Still, every February Latinos learn civil rights were invented by a Black man's dream. And Cesar Chavez, who was born in

Arizona, must struggle to be seen above Bud Light girls celebrating Cinco de Mayo, and the hateful speech dividing the country over "illegal" immigration.

When I hear the undocumented scapegoated as a threat to African-American livelihood, the problem is not just lack of mutual respect. *There is a financial interest invested in our lack of knowledge of each other.*

Who is who?
What's my name?
Is Brown the new Black?
It's not about who owns the bottom, but who's got my back.
Who. Represents. Me.

Blatinos in New York will tell you. Afro-Cubanos will tell you. Los Rakas will tell you. Soledad O'Brien. Daddy Yankee will tell you. Know the soul of black Peru mixed with indigenous like Tupac Amaru. Know that Africans are immigrants in Oakland, too. Know our common history.

The interdependence of Black and Brown is a reality now in Oakland, San Francisco, Salinas, Los Angeles. At every level Black and Brown need to be at the table representing and leading. Like Yanga. Like Guerrero. Like Martin and Cesar. If we are all going to thrive we have to represent and ri-i-i-i-de together.

Los Comemierda en SF (after La gran burguesia by Roque Dalton)

For Josué Rojas

The people in line at the taquería on Chestnut Street
in the Marina District
who say these tacos are just as good
as the Mission.

The people who chant,
All Lives Matter
at the Black Lives Matter rally.

The people on Facebook
Who argue
I have to look at pictures of your
kid's fifth grade graduation party
So, you can't complain about pictures of my pasta dinner
or pictures of my vacation
pictures of my outfits.

The people who cut funding for health care
Then pay for hospital marquees in their name.

The people who ban books
but are given Presidential libraries.

The people who tell you it's going to be great.
You're going to love it.
It's fantastic.
We have the best.

The most tremendous.
You gotta buy it from MyPillow

The people who put that comemierda in the White House.

The people who give you a porta-potty
a FEMA tent
two soggy slices of bread
wilted lettuce
and white cheese for catering.
Call it a music festival with a Jah Rule playlist
or Kenny Chesney playlist
or Blink 182 playlist.

Comemierda playlist.

The people who believe science was God-given.

The people still looking for weapons of mass destruction.
Still blaming Saddam for 9/11
The people who can't understand
why someone would blow themselves up
in a crowd for martyrdom
and heavenly afterlife.

The people who shout inside their masks.

The people who recall schoolboard members with corporate
          money
and demand the City reimburse the special election.

The people who turn back the clock

so they can live longer
while the rest of us burn.

These are the people who lose the most.

GHOST POEMS

My First Language Is Love

When my mother spoke Spanish to me
I was her mijo
I was her querido
I was her amor

My mother's Spanish
Saved me from loneliness
Saved me from feeling sorry for myself
When I felt embarrassed to explain my name
When they asked me, *Where are you from?*
When they asked me, *What are you?*

When I said Mexican
When I said Cuban
When people looked at me *like that*
When I smiled back
When they understood that I was loved
That I was not alone
That Spanish is my mother
my tías
my grandmother
mi abuelita
"¡Ay que lindo!"
My mother's voice so wonderful to hear
So, I never felt alone

Spanish is my mother tongue
My first language is love

When my mother spoke Spanish to me
I was her mijo
I was her querido
I was her amor

Spanish was our private
blood language battling
forced assimilation
My mother's Spanish lives
where my blood rushes between
Tolteca and Conquistador
Dreams and world war
Deep in my heart
they sound the same

In Ixtli In Yóllotl
Face and Heart
I look back and bring forth what's good
Cara y Corazón
Courage and Tenderness
I leave the pain of past generations
behind
I find the courage to go on

My mother was a healer.
When my teammate fell
on the second base path
dirt collecting in his tears,
he couldn't move his ankle.
"Me duele el tobillo."
Teammates, coaches, parents
all called for my mother

to come translate.
She became a healer.

My mother learned to love a white man
and even taught him Spanish, también.

Spanish is my mother tongue
My first language is love.

Mutation out of fragmentation
My mother's Spanish was a kaleidoscope
My identity became poetry
I turned in my rosary
for a Spanglish mandala of hope

My mother's tongue is Spanish
My first language is love

Bruce Lee at the Aero Drive-In

My father showed up one night
at my grandparents' house
to take me to the drive-in movie

A humid summer evening in El Cajón
My father's car crackled
over the gravel lot of the Aero Drive-In
as he parked next to the short pole
with a grey metal speaker attached

My father's thick pale wrist
reached through the half-rolled window
cigarette dangling from his lips
a beer between his legs
as he unlatched the metal speaker from the pole
and attached it to the driver side window

My father took a sip of his Michelob
and the movie sparked to life
The metallic sounds of fighting
filled the car
Bruce Lee appeared on the outdoor screen
battling kung fu challengers
and corrupt Chinese masters
Enter the Dragon
the first movie I saw with bloody violence
and naked women
The first movie I saw with my father

I was seven years old
Hadn't seen my father in a couple years
I didn't say much
The entire night I never moved in my seat
Never asked for candy or popcorn or soda
Not because I was afraid to ask my father
but because the movie was so intense

My attention was riveted by Bruce Lee
This man in the car with me
Emanating some power in his seat
My father
The movie
My father
The man
My father
The myth
The focus
The swagger
The dance and speedy power of Bruce Lee
I couldn't peel my eyes for two hours

My father just sipped his beer
Smoked his cigarette
And cackled every once in a while
at what a bad ass Bruce Lee was

When it was over, he drove me back
to my grandparent's house
It was late and just before he dropped me off,
he asked,
"So, what did you think of the movie?"

"I loved it," I said.
"Don't tell your ma.
She might get mad at me.
She'd never take you to see something like this."

So, I told my mother he took me
to see the Bruce Lee movie, anyway.

"So typical of your father to do that," she said.
"I won't forgive him for taking
a seven-year-old to an R-rated movie."

It was one of the greatest
examples of character
he ever gave me

The flying fists
The sweet science
The long stare
The violent dance
The labyrinth of mirrors
The self like water flow
The game inside the game
The teacher and the pupil
The philosophy

"What was silent in the father,
speaks in the son."

For the Honor of Cochise

Play time alone
at my grandmother's house in El Cajón
The only child of my backyard imagination

Dressed as an Indian
in my grandmother's makeup
Shirtless with a red lipstick lightning bolt
painted on my chest
Bath towels pinned around my waist

Fashioning a bow and arrow out of shoestring
and broken plastic PVC pipe
I pulled from Abuelo's shed
Shooting twigs
broken from the apricot tree
at the oncoming cowboys near the fence

The Honor of Cochise
        Burning my blood like a hot Bonanza

From another big tree hung
the heavy red vinyl Everlast punching bag
My uncles and I took turns putting on
the boxing gloves
and pounding the bag till we tired

When it was my turn to punch
I would plunge my fists into it
imagining my father's ribs

Beating, trying to muster
the force to break through sand like steel

When my uncles weren't around
and I couldn't find the gloves
I pounded the bag harder
Until my bare hands bled
And I wondered at the blood between my fingers
How it happens so easily
How you can bleed so easily
When you pound a heavy bag
That you wish was your father

Four Fathers

When I was nine years old
my mother decided to marry a man
with a red beard.

Abuelo Enrique said,
"Never trust a man with a beard.
He may be hiding something.
Cortez had a beard.
And you remember
what happened to Cuauhtémoc,
don't you?"

I kept looking for signs of insincerity,
but only found my stepfather's
Viking grin, a staple of his
"Old Time" personality.
He loved drinking Jack Daniels
and tooling around with his 1946 Roadster
more than me or my mother.

Four years later, we left the trimmed suburbs
for a two-bedroom apartment,
Chef Boyardee,
and coin laundry on Sunday.
I never asked my mother why
we gave up financial security,
or a middle-class nuclear family
and a house with two stories.
But I had a feeling

some prophecies are self-fulfilling.

I'm sure my mother had found out
the ugly truth
about the bearded Viking,
but chose to let me figure out
what type of man I would become:
Would I choose to grow a beard
or not.

> My own father was a phantom
> A wannabe philosopher
> Who only called
> when he was inspired.
> He wrote dense letters
> packed like cigarettes with epistemology
> that burned my image of a man
> into an ashtray.
> He was not an Indian.
> But he still couldn't grow a beard,
> or a bank account to save his life.

One day your acquaintances
might only be the people who serve you drinks.
You will smell like old newspaper and damp corduroy.
And you will only be held to account by the poetic solitude
of your fatherless insecurities.

Because now you have a son.
And he wants to walk
        more like run
hallway to the door, back and forth,

but he is not yet one.
His kneecaps are still developing.
So, he falls and bangs his head on the hardwood floor,
howling at the pain
and the fright of falling.

I act like nothing happened,
as if I could fool him out of his tears.
But my son is looking at me like I am a bully.
And something inside tells me he's right.

      I could be gone.
      I could disappear
      looking to find myself,
            the man I was supposed to be.
      Gone looking for God
      Gone looking out for number one
      Gone to write
            My days of solitary adventure/
            corner stacks of dog-eared books,
            a pot of cold coffee
            cigarette smoke and sandwich meat.

      I could grow a beard.
      Persuade myself
      that this is what sacrifice
      and personal freedom really look like.

But I want my son to trust the traits I carry.

I want to be present
to pick him up from his howling place.

I want him to sympathize
and understand
what dignity in the place of pride,
what responsibility in the place of attitude
what a macho really looks like.

Then I kiss his hands.
I kiss his knees.
and I kiss his feet.

So, he knows that men can be trusted not to leave, too.

Pepsi Kiss

I was twelve years old
The first time
Standing on her doorstep
saying goodbye to Cassandra
before her mamá called her in
from the block

She put her arms around my neck
I went numb everywhere
Except my mouth
Where her tongue flipped mine over
I thought I heard waves crashing on the shore
Until I noticed I spilled the can of Pepsi
I had been holding
While we were kissing
It was soda running over my Vans

She giggled and said goodbye
But Cassandra held my twelve-year-old life in her kiss
I stood there frozen
In a pool of fizzled brown soda
Unable to recognize myself

Two weeks later she went for the older dude
across the street
skater boy
fourteen with the golden hair
who could fight
to show he wasn't no punk

They kissed in front of me
in his front yard
after a game of two-on-two football

I went home and played Michael Jackson
"She's Out Of My Life"
over and over in my room
and cried that humid
never-ending summer.

Position No. 2 on Your Line-up Card (Make Your Mother Proud)

They told me the quickest way
to get signed was behind the plate
So, they put my best weapon on defense
And I dawned the tools of ignorance
Mask, chest protector, shin guards
Made me a catcher

Quickest way to the pros
was to catch
You should have seen me play
You should have seen me
I had a gun
On my shoulder
Full metal jacket
Couldn't steal on me
I gunned them down
My elbow a trigger
When they'd run,
I'd pull it
Blam!
Dead ducks on a pond
Wouldn't steal on me again

I knew they were watching me
Scouting me, studying me
since I was fifteen
The pro scouts used to
chat up my mom

Pretty brown lady
in sunglasses
red pumps and a business dress
just off work
Pretty brown lady standing
behind the backstop
arms crossed tensely
Sunglasses hiding
Beaming eyes
Shaking her leg
Nylons vibing
Poppin' her gum
Anxiously waiting
for her boy
to call the pitch
throw them out
and hit the ball

These scouts would sweat my mom
Talking about a better future
for her boy
They wished they knew my mother
Whistled with two fingers in her mouth
Could hear her over the crowd,
"C'mon, baby. You can do it."
Really
I played for her

To swing for her
Bend the knees
Tuck your chin
Swivel hips

Straight to the ball
Letters that pitch
Watch for the curveball in the dirt
Curveball in the dirt
Curveball in the dirt
Damn!
Lay off that shit
See your pitch
Swing
Swing
Swing
Two hundred swings a day
for my mom
Work like my mom
Every day for mom
Block fifty balls in the dirt
Long toss
Running poles
Left to right
Again and again
like writing a script

I wanted to change our story
I wanted to make money playing ball
Make money on my own
Make my mother proud
Give her an early retirement
Pay her bills
Get her a house
Be an example
Get an education
Get their attention

Let them know
My mother did this
all on her own
Raised me
without a husband
Molded me into the best
She taught me the game
To love the game like she did
Unconditionally.

She made me a ball player
Discipline and sacrifice
She spent her vacations on me
Drove miles to see my games
She put in work
to get me to practice
So, my practice got fierce
like my mother's relentless
punch of the clock
Rent is due
So, get to work

Her dedication to me
got me drafted by the Chicago Cubs
The team our whole family adored
My mom and her brothers and sisters
grew up just outside Chicago
Used to take the train to Wrigley Field
to watch Ernie Banks, Billy Williams, and Ron Santo

Then the Chicago Cubs were in my apartment
negotiating a contract with me

my mom and my uncle
I ate it up. Was so excited
I would have played for the Cubs
for pride alone
I was itching to sign the contract
and get my uniform
with my name on the back
For my family
For my mother
The scout knew it
Tried to lowball me
stalling and threatening lost opportunity.
But my uncle called him on it
They had to match a full ride scholarship to a D1
So, he added another zero to the check
And just before midnight
I signed the contract

The next morning, I flew to Mesa, AZ.
For spring training
I got paid more money
than I had ever seen in my life.
I was 19.
I made my mother proud.

What do you leave behind when you depart?

A bouquet of stargazers on the bed
A scent discovered in her favorite color
A precious note, a reminder
A promise I never intend to break

Dishes drying on the rack
45 inches of laughter folded into a red teddy bear blanket
Spider-Man rainboots at the foot of his bed
Cereal bar crumbs in the couch

Oscar D'León on the stereo
Songs that clackety-clack off wood floors
Salsa circles in the living room
A grey sweater,
Smells of her perfume.

All lights off
because even though
she's scared of the dark,
she can't tolerate waste.

The Solamar Hotel

Pink sun-dripped balcony
amid black breaks like lace hearts
over the hotel alarm
clock's digital torture.

I'm lying across the bed
with half a glass of dark rum
sweating on an end table
mystery of you
looping through my mind
with Maxwell's *Bad Habits*.

This is the highest cost.
Take you and make you off.

After years of making with you
my stomach never fails to knot
waiting for you to come.
My blood cells are still
resurrecting themselves
since the first time we made love.

I can't control the feeling.
The past is not dead.
This memory not a corpse.
It's a bad habit.
Jouissance
A curse to remember.
Then neglect.

Because I'd die for this.
Satisfaction is a myth.
Pleasure is pain
played again and again.

You change beyond tempting
and hard for me to keep repose.
My body wants to levitate.
And cling to your curves
temple inviting me to tantric divinity.

You sit on top of me
drink the brown liquor,
suck the ice, clasp my face
and quench my tongue.
Your breath is icy hot.
Your neck, elaborate
stargazers with citrus.
I want to taste the flower.

Like a cliff diver measuring the fall
before he breaks the dark shimmering surface
I jump off.
You know the danger of the reef.
All beauty is the beginning of terror.

Relax.
Just lay back.
This is all for you.

Up close feminine architecture
from this perspective is intricate

complexity suffocating me.
Blood beating in our throats and groins.
We devour time like Aztec gods.
Uncovered, syncretized serpent idols
consuming each other underneath Sea and Sun.
Our climax is thrown
with our garments.
Room service won't pick up this mess.

The clock is frozen at 10:36.
All is quiet and moonlit
as you crawl into my hollow
to rest your cheek on my chest.
I feel like my soul just had a stroke
and woke six years later
sore after we broke up.

This memory is worth the pound of flesh.
As it slides down my spine,
tiptoes out to the balcony,
and flies into the pulsating
ocean mist mixed with dim light.

I inhale it all back...

Ghost Poem

Didn't I feel unloved already before I knew what love was?

No one likes to deal with heartbreak

Wonder if you should shoot yourself sometimes

Knowing it's gone

                    Broken

        from the inside

                Family is broken

        from the inside

Not what you had dreamed it would be

Children won't see you in bed together anymore

No family heirlooms to pass down to grandchildren

No family photos on the walls

No family vacations anticipated

No long anniversary gatherings

Divorce for one child
Means the other is either
In crisis or
No part of the solution
The reason must be
Balance is burden
Come together now all
For forced codependence

Single parenting feels like raising a ghost family

Not what you dreamed it would be

    Broken

      from the inside

        out

Like someone poked a tiny hole in your balloon

      from the inside

        out

          A slow deflation

A slow spinning airless chamber

            A slow death

And you will cry

La Llorona invites you

baptizes you in ghost tears

too heavy to float

the ghost in you

invites her embrace

Ready to attach yourself to

someone to sleep

on the cold side of the bed

Nobody is clean and free of heartbreak

No one escapes the past

Isn't everybody wounded?

Isn't every relationship an effect of the one before?

Didn't my father leave me?

Didn't he break my heart already?

Didn't I feel unloved already before I knew what love was?

No one likes to deal with a broken heart

Prayer to Sleeping Grandmother (Cerro Pedernal, New Mexico)

For Jimmy Santiago Baca

This morning near Ghost Ranch
I hike to the foot of the sleeping grandmother
I pray with an ancient
New Mexican Tehua spirit
And the ashes of Georgia O'Keeffe
resting atop the mesa of Cerro Pedernal
in the heart of the dry river basin

Over rocks, looking for arrowheads
and rattlesnakes
Ancestors bracing my steps
Red and grey cliffs crowning me
Voices of the birds surrounding me
persuading me to lay my carga
at the foot of the sleeping grandmother

Grandmother hold my heart

Grandmother bring me peace

Grandmother help me raise my children
with courage to be who I am
to stand strong in my home
as a father should

Grandmother speak to me like the thunder

Grandmother bring me medicine
to withstand the storm

Grandmother strike lighting in my pen
Give me the voice
to show my children the struggle
to be a father has given me purpose

Grandmother let this creativity come
like mountains returning my echo
My responsibility to feed
Open mouths waiting at my table
My children surrounding me

WE STILL BE

21st Century Performance Poems

We Still Be

For Norman Zelaya

My empire of fog-crowned hills
Through webs of electric Muni lines
That tang of Philz roasted coffee grinds
Scorched breath of San Francisco poets
Emits passion of Juana Alicia, Roberto Vargas,
and Juan Felipe Herrera
Legacy of Ginsburg, Kaufman, and Diane di Prima
Devotion to its exotics, its unions,
rituals, and gangster politics

Where a dancer can steal your heart
and hold it for ransom at a gallery called
Crucible Steel   This muse
More than just an obsession
More like a blood oath to embrace Carnaval
Where even the most strait-laced
          will cross-dress
                    for the sake of adventure

This is San Francisco's heartbeat
This is San Francisco's heartbeat

My homie's house burned down
and we read poetry in the ashes
We raised some cash and his spirits
with bottles of tequila and Coronas
Salted tears to quench harsh throats
We told jokes and Marcus played hard be-bop

My homie wailed for his dog
lost in the smoke of a broken
pilot light-induced inferno

Poetry heals, the be-bop revives
Poetry heals and the be-bop revives
We never, we never, we never go softly
into that dark night

This is San Francisco's heartbeat
This is San Francisco's heartbeat

They say Blacks and Mexicans
don't belong anymore
Can't afford to raise a family
in a decent size home, anymore
But Muni drivers are Black
(those jobs last forever)
Latino teachers got white kids speaking Spanish
until Chicano becomes a four-letter word

If you peel the flyers from the telephone poles
you'll find broadsides protesting
gentrification of the guayabera
nineteen twenty-one, or twenty nineteen-year-olds
My broadsides were bilingual when it was illegal

They don't know how to stop this flow
A poetry evangelist with contraband
Mexican cigarettes by the pound
Yo soy Delicado.
We liberated public space con queso

Con el tambor y el chekeré
Con bass y saxophone
Con Jimmy Biala y David Molina
Con Howard Wiley and Marcus Shelby
With Jon Jang and Genny Lim
and Rho-Dessa-Jones

With bourbon and rum
and smoke and drum
With bourbon and rum
and smoke and drum
We took maní crudo to the toolshed
And we made *relámpago negro*
That's black lightning
Enrique Quique Padilla
Relámpago Negro!

This is San Francisco's heartbeat
This is San Francisco's heartbeat

People always want to know
What's so good about San Francisco?

It's the poets
It's the poets
It's the poets
It's the crazy
                drunk
                    loud ass
                        poets
                        from the Mission
The Fillmore

The Bayview
North Beach
Hunter's Point
I wasn't born here, but I ain't no tourist
And I know my way around

Broke so many hearts
But keep coming back for more
We speakeasy at Bruno's in the corner of the bar
Her style is Latin swing
with strapless dress and high heels
She brown skin so beautiful
Want her to wear my ring
Represent her swagger
with mestizo babies in the sling
We Jazz Fest in North Beach
with tapas on the grass
We festival in Stern Grove
We Carnaval
We Baker Beach
Our babies growing so fast
And we like to show them off
on FacebookTwitterInstagramSnapchat
LinkedInGooglePlus
The Bay Area got them all.

San Francisco is our heart
Many have come to claim her throne
Many moved to Oakland
Home is where I'm loved the most

So, rise San Francisco

Like a trolley train over Pacific Heights
We look to you for inspiration
when life is about struggle
You make it possible to desire something different
You make it possible to believe
Because we still believe
We still believe
We still believe
Yes, we still believe
Yes, we still be

We still be
We still be
We still be

The heartbeat of San Francisco

SURVIVAL BOAT

Inspired by photographer Moses Slovatizki

This is the hull of the boat
from what once was tree trunk
cut into vessel beached on sand
in front of a cobalt blue wall
on the shore in Puerto Rico

This is the texture of human labor
An immigrant's dream with sharp angles
like scales of a wooden whale
carved with hand-held chisel
to assure the delivery of promises to family

This is arrival by sea.

This is the tradition of native Tainos
who travelled freely
between Caribbean islands
before Columbus arrived.

This is after that.

This is the result of that landing
Descendants of indigenous people
still striving against state policies
to build a home for their families

The people who carved this boat
left the Dominican Republic

crossed the sea
and secretly landed on Puerto Rico
in search of abundance
on ancestral lands
called Borinken
This is Native American culture
of the Antilles islands
indigenas antillanos
A journey across aqua borders

This is hope that we will win.
This is an investment in our future.
This is a 700-year-old family heirloom.

This is a picture of a boat proving
the value of indigenous people
Endures
The dream of family
survives
Promises remembered and delivered

This is a boat

Cayuco, Canoa, Canoe
Cayuco, Canoa, Canoe

We are bound to the water
From trees to men navigating on the
ocean
Everyone comes from another land

We've been here for thousands of years

I brought a lot of sand
from the bottom of the sea

I've come to meet my family
Meet my brothers and sisters
Tainos. Arawak. Caribs

All these islands are my home
I brought a lot of sand
from the bottom of the sea

Oh God, don't let me drown
before I reach shore
My family needs me
I left my daughter behind
to find work and food

We will share it all
From trees to men navigating on the ocean
Everyone comes from another land
I brought a lot of sand
from the bottom of the sea

700 Days (Lorena's Poem)

Inspired by Las Madres de Berks by Michelle Angela Ortiz

ICE put Lorena
and her 2-year-old son Gabriel
in an immigrant detention prison
for 22 months—
700 days the little boy's
memory began while locked up
playing ball with his toddler inmates
at Berks Family Prison in Pennsylvania.

ICE put Lorena
and her 2-year-old son Gabriel
in an immigrant detention prison
for 22 months, 700 days

At the end, the Federal judge asked the prosecutor:
"What is a four-year-old child doing in prison for 700 days?"
The Federal Prosecutor could not respond.

Lorena and Gabriel came from Honduras.
She crossed the border with her child
to seek asylum from domestic violence.
She did not steal.
She did not murder.
She did not run from the authorities.
Still, ICE put Lorena and her 4-year-old son in prison
for 22 months, 700 days in Berks, Pennsylvania.

Today, 111 immigrant children are still held behind bars.

Most of them under 5 years old,
and for extra-long stays.

"What is a four-year-old child doing in prison for 700 days?"

In Berks Family Residential Center-prison
There's no school
So, guards teach the children
to speak English with, "Shut up and be quiet."
Lorena asked her lawyer, *what did that mean?*
Callate.
Shut up. Be quiet.
Children are being too loud in prison
playing games—It's too much
for guards to learn to say a Spanish phrase.
So, *shut up and be quiet* will be your lesson today.

"What is a four-year-old child doing in prison for 700 days?"

People donated $25 million
GoFundMe to build a wall at the Mexican border
Steven Bannon took that money on vacation.

They spent $14 billion on the election
But they said it was a fraud.

It was President Obama and Biden
built those cages,
where immigrant children slept on the ground
with an aluminum blanket
and two sandwiches a day.
I thought people elected Joe Biden

because they said they wanted a change.

"What is a four-year-old child doing in prison for 700 days?"

They deported Gabriel's four-year-old friends
from Berks Family Prison.
They lost the parents of over 600 children
and forced them into the foster system.
Here's where my tax money goes.

When the judge saw four-year-old Gabriel
after 700 days in a cell
he said Lorena and her son
could live with a family sponsor
while their asylum is decided.

ICE put a GPS collar on Lorena's ankle
and let her free of Berks Family Prison in Pennsylvania.
Freedom by any means
Freedom by any ways
and whoever pays

I'm sending my tax return to the Shut Down Berks Coalition
        because

"What is a four-year-old child doing in prison for 700 days?"

José Feliciano: Only in America

For Jon Jang

You are a child of Lares, Puerto Rico
Mixed with Rock, Soul, the Delta Blues
An American Folk Music legend

José Feliciano
You came to New York when you were five
Learned to play guitar at nine
A teenager during the Great Folk Scare
Coming of age in Greenwich Village
In the early 1960's with Bob Dylan

A Puerto Rican teenager
alone on stage with your acoustic guitar
You passed the hat at the cafes, clubs, and bars
after your sets for a salary
to help your family

The sighted world tried to pigeonhole you.
They didn't know your mother taught you
to be independent as a child
Not to be afraid of the dark
No fear of isolation

José, can you see?
This land is their land
This is white, man
This Land is White Man?
This land you're alien.

Your heart has always been a bright light
Because we feel your voice when you sing, José
You wailed the covers off popular songs
performing in Spanish *and* English
so the radio *couldn't* ignore you.

At 21 you went to Argentina
Adding the blues and folk influences
to the Spanish boleros and torch songs
The music had to be melancholic
to reflect the loneliness
being a blind Latino genius
in a privileged sighted world

In Latin America
you found the secret of your style;
But you really loved American music.
Then 1968 you came back
with your rendition of The Doors' "Light My Fire"

It was your first official "crossover" hit.
An acoustic songwriter Latinizing rock songs.
You were opening for 'Old Blue Eyes'
Frank Sinatra in Las Vegas.
Your voice brought ease to troubled hearts
like a moonlit walk on the beach
for a nation at war with Vietnam,
and at war with itself.

Until they invited you to Detroit
In October of 1968

to sing the National Anthem
during game five of the World Series.

Twenty-three years old
in center field of Tiger Stadium
A full band of white musicians to back you up.
But you didn't need them.
Told them you would play this solo.
Just you and your guitar.
The American flag waving high behind you.
And you began to sing a soulful cry
A cry for hope, unity, and freedom.

José can you see?
As you beautifully bent the notes towards freedom
Grito de Lares rising through your throat
You were Bob Dylan, Joan Baez, Harry Belafonte.
Your dark glasses made you a thug
Your long dark hair made you a dirty hippy
Reminded the baseball crowd of Anti-war protest
Folk Scare.

It was 1968 the most revolutionary year in America's modern
            history.
You sang the National Anthem different.
Made us feel more entitled to its promise.
Made us feel like the anthem could be a song for *all of us*.
And for that, they hated you.

Only in America.

José could you feel?

Baseball fans reacted with a chorus of boos and outrage.
They attacked your performance of The Star-Spangled Banner
as disrespectful, anti-American, and unpatriotic.
They called for you to be deported.
They didn't know Puerto Ricans are American citizens.

Only in America

They pulled your records off the radio
And for three years your recordings were blacklisted
and banned.

Only in America

José Feliciano
American folk music legend
One of the most difficult songs to sing
You made the Anthem yours
By the way you sang it
We could all see.
Who really matters in America?
Who has the courage to claim to be an American?

You could see the future:
Jimi Hendrix at Woodstock
Marvin Gaye at the NBA All-Star Game
Whitney Houston at the Super Bowl
All of them singing the American Anthem
their own personal way.
Like you did, José.

Then a couple years later

you made the country yours again
Now every Christmas we sign your song
Feliz Navidad
Another hit!

José, we can see you
All you have done
9 Grammys
60 albums
Hit singles

You changed the American Anthem.
Made us feel more entitled to its promise
Like it could be a song for all of us
You changed the National Anthem
by making it your own song.

Only in America

CAGES: A Way to Interrogate History

A jazz collaboration between Jon Jang and Paul S. Flores

Letter A

Music ensemble performs fast, dissonant passages

Letter B

NO MUSIC

Jazz music is really liberation music

: a way to interrogate history

Percussion punctuation

Letter C

Horns play 4 fast notes followed by a long tone

Chinese built the railroad

Wuhan cymbal struck 1 time

Japanese-American farmers in the West

Wuhan cymbal struck 2 times

After 8 beats by multiple percussion.

Mexican land is 1/4 of the US

Horns come in around there

1848 jack movements

After music ensemble stops

The border crossed us

Piano performs a slow short figure
Multiple percussion performs to give time to Jon to put on white mask

Letter D
Music ensemble mocks American marching band. Ends with ascending 3-note figure

Letter E

Whose America?

Repeat ascending 3-note figure

Stolen at gunpoint

Repeat ascending 3-note figure

Hunted at Walmart

for being brown in Texas

Club without a pulse in Orlando

a bloody concert in Las Vegas

Country music is no consolation

US music institutions are repressive and racist

Can't sing the National Anthem

Without pointing a gun

Repeat ascending 3-note figure

Whose notes are purposefully impossible for me to hiiiiiit?

Letter F
Music ensemble performs fast dissonant passages
After saxophone and trombone enters

Jazz breaks me out of racial oppression.
Jazz is a slave name

Letter G
NO MUSIC

Black people did not call it jazz

: a way to interrogate history

Letter H
Saxophone, trombone, piano bass perform 4 notes followed by a long tone

1882 Chinese Exclusion Act

Saxophone, trombone, piano bass perform 4 notes followed by a long tone

1908 Chinese Paper Sons rise like the Phoenix
Jang born out of the Great San Francisco earthquake
and Woo burned in the fire

Saxophone, trombone, piano bass perform 4 notes followed by a long tone

Who? Jang. Woo? Jang. Who? Jang. Woo? Jang.

1910 Angel Island Chinese Detention Center
intensive traumatic interrogations
in 1914, 1916, 1921, 1933 and 1934.

Saxophone, trombone, piano bass perform 4 notes followed by a long tone

Letter I
NO MUSIC

1942 Japanese incarceration—
Many Japanese-Americans were incarcerated in concentration
camps without due process
Tanforan Mall used to be a racetrack
Government transformed the horse stables to imprison
thousands of innocent Japanese-Americans
1945 released from prison camps in Arizona only to live in a
renovated chicken coup

Letter J
Bowed bass (arco), piano, multiple percussion performs slow eerie music

2014 Obama Administration built the Customs and Border
Patrol Central Processing Center to hold 1500 Central
American immigrants in Texas

The Border Patrol used chain link fence to separate men from
women and children

Letter K
Ensemble performs Max Roach's "It's Time"

A section

American in CAGES ONLY

2ⁿᵈ time A section

American in CAGES ONLY

B section

2018 President Trump Zero Tolerance Immigration Policy
separated babies and children from their mothers
Children in cages by themselves, before deporting their
mothers.

Letter L
A section

American in CAGES ONLY

B section

For the sons of Paper Sons who fly too close to the sun

For the sons of Paper Sons who got good jobs

Can afford to fly across country in the 1950s
Can afford to buy a house in the suburbs
But still must be interrogated first by the FBI
Senator Joe McCarthy doesn't believe in Chinese-American
success

For the sons of Paper Sons who fly too close to the sun

His Jewish friend and coworker had to buy the house for him
Chinese still couldn't buy a house in an all-white neighborhood

For the sons of Paper Sons who fly too close to the sun

There's always a fire to fall from

Letter M
NO MUSIC

People are on boats
People clinging to planes
Crossing the desert to survive

13,000 Black Caribbeans and Haitians living under a bridge
in Mexico waiting to cross the Rio Grande
into Del Rio, Texas

The border patrol on horseback
Waiting for them on the other side

Letter N
Saxophone & trombone perform slow 3-note figures

We build a wall to keep us free
We build a wall to keep us free

American in CAGES ONLY

Ace of Wands

For Adrian Arias

When it's your turn to receive
the vaccine
Don't throw away your shot

Teachers still waiting
To be truly appreciated
55,000 students hope to leave
the screen for the
      senior lawns or testing sites
          Vending machines full of hand sanitizer
and blue surgical masks
        instead of dry-packaged snacks

Imagination is a creative muscle
It needs to be worked out

Let conflict be your guide
Not fear of being left out
Not fear of being wrong
The truth is now the time
Every student is a potential teacher

Fear of losing creativity
Imagination is part of the natural world
Change is opportunity

Fear of history too comfortable
for students to vaccinate
their racist namesakes from the marquee

Before Padlets become pistols
No face
No case

If circumstances dictate
To improvise in a pandemic
Let the wand shake in the sky

PUBLICATION CREDITS

Thank you to following publications in which these poems previously appeared in similar or different forms.

"Spanglish" first appeared in *Palabras de Poder: Rebel Writers from the New Latin@ America*, Chapbook, ed. Cal A. Vera, 2008, Red Calacarts Publications.

"Crowbar Thing," first appeared in *La Lunada: An Anthology of Spoken Word Poetry Celebrating Sixty Full Moons and Community Ritual and Galeria de la Raza*, ed. Marc Pinate, 2010, Galería de la Raza, San Francisco, CA. Also appeared in *Me No Habla With Acento*, ed. Emanuel Xavier, 2011, Rebel Satori Press and Museo Del Barrio, NYC.

"Chicano Supernova," "Sidewalk Librarian," and "Arroz Con Pollo" first appeared in *Me No Habla With Acento*, ed. Emanuel Xavier, 2011, Rebel Satori Press and Museo Del Barrio, NYC.

"Brown Dreams" first appeared in *The Rain*, Chapbook, 2003 (Paul S. Flores, Cho Cho Chocoyo Press). Also appeared in *Me No Habla With Acento*, ed. Emanuel Xavier, 2011, Rebel Satori Press and Museo Del Barrio, NYC. Also appeared in *Rhythm and Resistance: Teaching Poetry for Social Justice*, ed. Linda Christensen and Dyan Watson, 2015, Rethinking Schools Ltd.

"Gravity's Volume" first appeared as "Dedication to Geoffrey Canada: The Gravity and the Volume" in *Journal of Critical Thought and Praxis*, Volume 1, Issue 1, October 2012, Iowa State University, IA.

"Four Fathers" first appeared in *Me No Habla With Acento*, ed. Emanuel Xavier, 2011, Rebel Satori Press and Museo Del Barrio, NYC.

"We Still Be," "Survival Boat," "700 Days (Lorena's Poem)," "Jose Feliciano: Only in America," and "CAGES: A Way to Interrogate History," will all appear on the jazz recording "CAGES: Ways to Interrogate History with Jon Jang and Paul Flores" on AsianImprov Records in 2023.

"Ace of Wands" first appeared in *Tarot in Pandemic and Revolution*, ed. Adrian Arias, 2021, Nomadic Press.

ACKNOWLEDGMENTS

Love to the live spots and humans that gave me a mic, a stage, a check and saw me come up and into this poetry over the last two decades. Ours is a communal poetics: Los Delicados, Youth Speaks, La Peña Cultural Center, Galería de La Raza, Acción Latina, Nuyorican Poets Café, SF Jazz, Asian Pacific Islander Cultural Center, Museo Del Barrio, Su Teatro, MECA-Houston, Xicanindio Artes, NALAC, National Performance Network, Chicano Messengers of Spoken Word, The Loft Literary Center, Teatro Milagro, Tigertail Productions, MACLA-San Jose, Grito Serpentino, The Taco Shop Poets, Voz Alta, Café on A, The Literary Café (Miami), Guadalupe Cultural Arts Center, A Mic and Dim Lights, Cuba Caribe, SFIAF, USF, Calaca Press, Baktun 12, Alliance for Boys and Men of Color, The Unity Council, Amy Cheney, Lit Crawl, Gala Hispanic Theater, LATC, CASA 0101, Community Works West, William James Association, National Compadres Network.

David A. Romero and Matt Sedillo for pushing their vison forward and including me in El Martillo.

My mother Patricia Flores-Magallanes. My children Santos Flores-Garcia, Luna Flores-Garcia, Joaquin Flores-Gallegos and their mothers. My grandmother Olga Rosa, my grandfather Enrique Flores-Garcia. Flores fam. Stojsavljevic fam. Summer Rogers.

Artist Fam:

Juan Felipe Herrera, Sandra Garcia, Kamilah Forbes, Aya de León, Marc Bamuthi Joseph, James Kass, Jason Mateo, Joan Osato, Sean San José, Rafael Casal, Bao Phi, Emmanuel Ortiz, Will "Da Real One" Bell (RIP), Emanuel Xavier, José Torres-Tama, Willie Ney, Marc David Pinate, Amalia Ortiz, Tomás Riley, Adrian Arancibia, Moses Slovatizki, Lizz Huerta, Amanda Quintero, Josué Rojas, LaTasha Nevada Diggs, Norman Antonio Zelaya, Darren J. de Leon, Chuy Quintero, Jaime Cortez, J. Andrea Porras / yAyA, Avotcja, Ric Salinas, Herbert Siguenza, Río Yañez, Jimmy Santiago Baca, Maxine Chernoff, Mary Luft, Alice Valdez, Andrew Wood, Tony Garcia, Rosalba Rolón, Alvan Colón Lespier, Anjee Helstrup-Alvarez, Dolores Huerta, Lupe Mendez, Lizbeth Ortiz, Vincent Toro, Jimmy Biala, Quique Padilla, Marcus Shelby, Genny Lim, Jon Jang, Yosvany Terry, DJ Leydis, Ramón Ramos Alayo, Mayda Del Valle, Elier "El Brujo" A. Alvarez, Paul Chin, Bobby LeFebre, Luz de Cuba, Roberto Gutièrrez Varea, Fatima Ramirez, Josiah Luis Alderete, Tongo Eisen-Martin, Michele Marie Serros (RIP), Bocafloja, Danny Hoch, Magia Lopez, Alexei Rodriguez, John and Mitzi Ulloa, Beth Boone, Sylvia Sherman, Julio Cárdenas, Yrak Saenz Orta, Edgaro, Gina Madrid, Elia Arce, Hodari Davis, Pat Payne, Aztlan Underground, Willie Perdomo, Adrian Arias, Maestro Jerry Tello, Aimee Suzara, Soldanela Rivera López, Rafael Flores, Jack Boulware, Macedonio Arteaga Jr., Arlene Biala, Rodrigo Sanchez-Chavarria, Michelle Angela Ortiz, José Manuel Martinez Gonzalez, John Santos, Yosimar Reyes, Alejandro Murguía, Juana Alicia, Tim Z. Hernandez, Roberto Vargas, Marc David Pinate, Milta Ortiz. To my first poetry teachers, Quincy Troupe and Victor Hernandez Cruz.

ABOUT THE AUTHOR

Photo by Tommy Lau

Paul S. Flores is one of the most influential Latino performance artists in the country and a nationally respected arts educator. He creates plays, oral narratives, and spoken word about transnationality and citizenship that spur and support societal movements that lead to change. Flores' ability to paint a vivid picture of the bi-cultural Latino experience is shaped by his personal background and experience growing up in Chula Vista, California, near the Mexican border. His body of work touches on the immigrant story in all its complexities: from the violent—forced migration, gang life, war, incarceration, and separated families—to zooming in on intergenerational relationships and the struggle of preserving important cultural values. As a San Francisco artist of Mexican and Cuban-American heritage, Paul S. Flores has built a national reputation for interview-based theater and bilingual spoken word. He integrates Latino and indigenous healing practices to tell the stories of real people impacted by immigration and systemic inequalities. Flores' work has played across the United States and internationally in Cuba, Mexico, and El Salvador. Paul is a Doris Duke Artist Award winner and an inaugural NALAC Catalyst for Change awardee. His commissions have come from Creative Capital, La Peña Cultural Center, MACLA, MAP Fund, Pregones Theater, National Performance Network, SF Arts Commission, Yerba Buena Center for the Arts and many more. Flores teaches Theater and Spoken Word at the University of San Francisco. He is a teaching artist in creative writing with the Prison Arts Project at CMF in Vacaville, and in San Quentin State Prison. He is the lead curator of Paseo Artistico Free Bilingual Community Art Stroll on 24th Street in the Mission District. He lives in San Francisco with his children.

paulsfloresart.com

ABOUT THE ARTIST

Xavi Moreno is a distinguished graphic designer & marketing consultant. Xavi built his marketing talent at a young age beginning with his first job at 10 years old helping to sell photos at weddings & quinceaneras for his photographer father, making and selling piñatas, to helping run the family-owned juice bar at age 13, and marketing design for one of the largest t-shirt manufactures in the world. Today, he is responsible for Company of Angels and The Los Angeles Theatre Center's innovative marketing. A sampling of Xavi's consulting and freelance clients include: American Apparel, Stussy, Urban Outfitters, Ford, Dr. Pepper, Vans & Jarritos. He was the 2011 Ford spokesperson for the Fiesta, "Ready Pa tu Mundo" campaign and quickly became an asset to the Ford Fiesta campaign, writing and performing the commercials for TV, radio, and internet. In 2013 he co-produced and was also 1 of 100 selected participants for the spectacularly successful "Fiesta Movement," a campaign that did an exceptional job of exposing the Fiesta name to a new generation of users gaining 6.2mm YouTube views, 750,000 Flickr views and 40mm Twitter impressions.

iamxavi.com

EL MARTILLO
PRESS

El Martillo Press publishes writers whose pens strike the page with clear intent; words with purpose to pry apart assumed norms and to hammer away at injustice. El Martillo Press proactively publishes writers looking to pound the pavement to promote their work and the work of their fellow pressmates. There is strength in El Martillo.

El Martillo Press launch 2023:

- *WE STILL BE: Poems and Performances*
        by Paul S. Flores
- *A Crown of Flames: Selected Poems & Aphorisms*
        by Flaminia Cruciani
- *Touch the Sky* by Donato Martinez
- *God of the Air Hose and Other Blue-Collar Poems*
        by Ceasar K. Avelar
- *the daughterland* by Margaret Elysia Garcia

To purchase these books and to keep up with new titles, visit elmartillopress.com.

Printed in the USA
CPSIA information can be obtained
at www.ICGtesting.com
LVHW010047171023
761252LV00003B/272